STATES OF AROUSAL

States of Arousal
by Sunshine O'Donnell

TRIO HOUSE PRESS

Copyright © 2023 Sunshine O'Donnell

No part of this book may be used or performed without written consent of the author, if living, except for critical articles or reviews.

O'Donnell, Sunshine
1st edition

ISBN:978-1-949487-09-1
Library of Congress Control Number: 2022949485

Interior design by Patrick Werle
Cover art by Louise DAlessandro
Cover design by Joel W. Coggins
Editing by Halee Kirkwood and Sarah Dumitrascu

Trio House Press, Inc.
Minneapolis
www.triohousepress.org

Table Of Contents

Lockdown	11
North Philly in August	15
Sinking	17
Show 'N Tell	18
what ache the pistons	20
Sudden Realization at the Age of 50 While Being Followed By a Man Who Tells Me Mmmm, You Look Good and is Waiting to Hear Thank You Which I Will Say So as to Avoid Making Him Angry	22
13-Year-Old Girls Impart Their Training After I Share My Sudden Realization	23
Attachment	26
Placement	30
Detachment	32
Pronouns	35
Screentime	36
COMPREHENSION QUIZ: Fun with the News on NPR!	38
How Can You Survive The End of the World?	40
Duck & Cover	42
You Notice Things	44
Analog Bulletins From 2002	47
State of Being	49

in the flesh   54

Plato's Hermaphrodite   56

ABSTRACT:

In this study, we investigate **arousal-activated adaptation towards pathologically reactive behaviors** in human subjects by validating three experimental conditions: (a) **unmonitored screen exposure** [necessary inclusions: bias-based violence, incestuous/pedophilic pornographic imagery, disjointed clips of extreme emotional affects {rage, bliss, terror}], (b) **consumption of addictive stimulants**, refined [for immediate absorption {e.g. cooked or extracted sugars, syrups in water, bleached flours}], and (c) **control scene:**

traumatic event[s], encroaching extinction.

Lockdown

*Where are we supposed to go if we have to run
away from the school?*

The first question of the day
from an eighth-grader whose mask
is crooked and
deliberately perched beneath
his nose, the only kind

of defiance he allows himself
now that the curve is flat. But he's
breathing

so hard the blue paper
soaks wet. Yesterday
we learned *Loss
of Innocence* and he had
wanted to know if it was good or
bad. Today

the Tik Tok challenge is clear:

National School Shooting Day
is this Friday.
The children crowd
me like pigeons.

*Your classroom is like
all glass, there's literally
nowhere to hide.*

In a Quaker School, our days
are punctuated by wholesome
silences, luminated
by real photons from the sun
through unbarred windows, precious

after decades of teaching

in basements and concrete
blocks, Philly public schools with signs
over each fountain: DO NOT DRINK
THE WATER.

*Here is the new
lock*, I say, *with a huge bolt
inside. No one can shoot through*. I show
them the thirty pound
typewriter by the door, the
birthday cake knife,
all of the things I know
how to weaponize. I say
*I will not let anyone
hurt you.*

They don't believe me.
They are always suspicious
now.
Aren't we the same adults

who gathered them, unmasked
on March 12th, said *We'll see you
soon!* and then watched those words
drag like ridiculous glaciers
for months? Haven't we
told them what they will
inherit? Heirlooms
of plastic and poisons, antibiotic
soil. A corona
of space trash halos the planet.

*What if we hear the shots
while we're playing outside?*

This is a Quaker school
in a town where roads get salted
and buildings repaired. The police do not
patrol halls between classes. The only
litter we see
 are masks discarded or dropped.

I tell them *We run to the Meetinghouse,*
that's our safe space
but I don't know
if this is true.

I don't know if anywhere will ever seem
safe again. They were in
kindergarten when Sandy Hook
happened. We did not tell the babies
that babies had been killed.

They are not
surprised anymore. Last week's school
shooting, no one noticed. Famous
grown-ups debate online, angry
about the gender of cartoon candies. We say

Pay attention
we ask *What*
do you notice?
and they tell the truth:
Everything is

broken.
But this boy is not broken
yet, only scared. I tell him, again, *fix*
your mask.

I want to say
it's all broken but you
are light that does not
break.

Instead, I show him
a closet good for hiding in, a table, a desk, and he
nods but his breathing does not
slow down.

We need drills, he says, *please*
and walks away, shifting
into a role that does not allow

for fear. He can
hide beneath humor and hoodies.
I've seen him camouflage

sadness this way. I foolishly wish
a cocoon to protect him, a magic
spell to repel
        virus
        bullet
        harm
knowing

that all of the losses
are already transcribed
into every cell.

North Philly in August

Scattered parasol branches, their

canopies shielding

blunt ends and bottles, how the

shards of glass glitter

by a curb that crumbles like cake.

The Ladies in Hats are still ladies and all

the boys bow, cussing suspended

till the Ladies sail past. The heat makes thick

their regality. The brave

stockinged legs and canes carefully

navigate the gutted path.

The Ladies do not sweat,

but the boys do. They peel off

giant white t-shirts and play, become

master hunters of shade. The walls

engorge with drowsy whorls

from old leaks and paint, the hot

bricks broken and ribbons

of paper that uncling

and curl, dipping

down past the choke vines and the heeled shoes, down past

the sacred procession, then down where elaborate

shadows have seeped

into the ground like oil.

Sinking

[There are neighborhoods throughout Philadelphia built on top of marshland. Many of these began to sink catastrophically in the 1990s]

a cartoon quicksand
that is not quick, a
shrugging vortex
eating its young,
submission by softness.
the children
don't know that they know
how everything is halved here.
the houses that still stand are split with
the stains
of ghost stairs or walls
the sparse and sick
trees submitting to pulses,
black plastic bags hung
like ornaments on every branch.
empty sugar-straws
tumbleweed across asphalt.
the wind sends sinuous
whispers like dry
waves or applause, a graceful
ovation growing
around all of the things that do not grow.
it surprises us with a sheltering
sound that is
not quite music or disguise,
but an alien health so
conspicuous
it settles its grace
before the doors
of all the upright houses.

Show 'N Tel

is one of the places where I sell stripper clothes with my dad
in the nineties. To get in,
we walk through a small shop that sells
reproductive organs made of rubber and silicone, then pass
the BYO *Full Nude Dance* room. Upstairs, girls perch
on stools, each in front of her own little booth. One of the girls
is so pregnant her golden-brown belly ball hides
the front of her g-string. It's noon and the whole building already
smells like turpentine. White businessmen on lunch break
skulk the halls to choose their girls while we set up our racks
and a teenage boy mops one of the rooms.
The "Tel" part is what makes it
legal. After you choose your girl and go into
the room, separated from her by a
Plexiglass wall, you use the old fashioned
phone on your side and tell her what
to do. Once
we heard a dog barking but it was just a naked
man being walked on a leash. My dad
and I hang the costumes for sale, chat with the girls who teeter over
on impossible heels. The fumes from the mop-boy's bucket will stay
in my hair for hours.
This club is different from the others we work. The "gentlemen's"
clubs
bring in the most money; the girls know how to persuade
the men to pay. The men
say stupid things to me.
You can tell the girls here are really into it.
Why aren't you up on that stage? You'd make a fortune.
They say this to me because I'm wearing
clothes. Barely, but enough
to be a good girl in this context, and therefore worth more
than the girls wearing nothing. Over and over again
I am offered money to dance. One owner sends me
jewelry and steak. Every day I consider
getting up on the stage. Backstage,
the girls peel off artifice and talk about
how much they hate the men. The girls
make retching sounds, say *they are fucking*

disgusting. The girls tell me
terrible things that happened to them when they were
little and then not so little. They say dancing for money
keeps them in control. They say none of it is real.
The money
is real, I watch it move from hand to body all night. At home,
I look at myself topless in the mirror and I am more naked
than anyone I've ever seen.

At Show 'N Tel, I feel sad
for the girls on their perches. I know how
they got here, but how will they get
out? At the end of a shift, wearing flip-flops and sweats, the girls
count their money and smoke. I help my father
break down racks, zip up big plastic bags full of clothes.
Without the foundation and clip-in extensions, the girls look
tired, older than they are. Some of them hug me
goodbye. They like me because I have clothes on
and I listen.

One day I go straight from Show 'N Tel
to interview a survivor from Auschwitz. She lets me into her rowhome
in the Northeast and tells me
how her boots saved her life. I worry she can smell
the floor cleaner fumes, but I'm grateful
to hear her story and I write
as quickly as I can. She shows me pictures
of her grandchildren, asks about my family.
She says *you do anything you got to do to survive.*

what ache the pistons

And stamens
Not requiring a slap or friction
But the small concentrated buzz
Of wings and mandibles gorging
Such public genitals shameless
On the kitchen table
Slatternly petticoats dropping
And forgotten as they die. To have
Underskirts that were once alive
And then aren't. For humans
This would mean surgery and
Illusion, silicone petals
And synchronized falling
And none of it covered by
Insurance. But the boys'
Buzzing and frantic
Nosing into parts, this
They would cover, a stimulant
Green and worth more than gold
Gilding noses and wings hysterical
Because they are too old
For the lovely dusts, the
Stickying down into the Ladies' parts
And relishing it, setting up camp
Among all the folds and furies.
Little do they know these
Boyscouts of the rich and fermented,
That almost-rotten is the moment
When things are most sweet.
They nuzzle like dogs
Into the offering, grateful
But not knowing why
Lost in the pistons, the stamens, the sticky
Reality of things. Because all they have
To give in the end is half a plan
And not even the
Best plan, just one plan
From billions, and never knowing
Which is going to win out, and

Probably not caring either way.
Such small, slow brains
Such lost, slow vertebrates.
Even the brightest. Even
The sweetest. These sad
And safe lost boys. Even our sweetest
Of sons. Even they
Will never know.

Sudden Realization at the Age of 50 While Being Followed by a Man Who Tells Me *Mmmm, You Look Good* and Is Waiting to Hear *Thank You*, Which I Will Say so as to Avoid Making Him Angry

I am prey

no matter how old

                                                            there is no aging
                                                            out

13-Year-Old Girls Impart Their Training After I Share My Sudden Realization

1.1 You Should Never:
    I. Go anywhere alone
    II. Leave your drink alone
    III. Wear your hair in a ponytail because they can yank from the back and pull you

2.1 If They Get You:
    I. In the trunk of a car, kick out the back lights and put your hand through
    so the car behind you can see your hand waving for help
    II. You have to yell "fire!" because if you yell "rape", no one will come
    IV. Never let them take you to a second location

3.1 When You Hear Footsteps Behind You:
    I. Pretend to be on the phone with your
        a. Brother
        b. Boyfriend
        c. Dad
    I. Facetime anyone so you can see who's behind you
    II. Keep pepper spray in your bag, especially when you take the bus
    III. Keep your keys between your fingers, poking out *

4.1 While Being Harrassed:
    I. When they tell you to smile, just smile and keep walking
    II. If they say something about you or what they'd like to do to your parts, do not say anything back

      III.   If they get mad because you don't say anything back, you can always run

5.1   **Be Prepared:**
      I.   Wear sneakers so that you can run
      II.   Wear baggy clothes so they can't see your body
      III.   Wear a hoodie so they think you're a boy
      IV.   Act crazy, make sounds and talk to yourself

6.1   **But Whatever You Do:**
      I.   Do not make him mad

---

*An ancient trick passed down from mother to daughter for generations, however:
it will not work as a weapon and may most likely enrage the man you are attempting to fight off. Choose this technique with caution.
Consider instead, asking a man you trust to escort you to your car. [1]

[1] This may prove to be, paradoxically, the wrong move, as the men you trust most are statistically more liable to assault in ways both soft [A.] and overt

---

[A.] Pressing too hard or too long against you during a hug, moving a hand on your back where your bra is connected, rubbing shoulder, arm, hip, or knee, saying evaluative things about your appearance. Here is when you should make your best attempt to fawn your way out of entrapment

---

Rarely taught yet most often used, fawning is the fourth F of stress responses. Freezing might be misread as consent, and something you will regret later [X]

[X] My own specialty is to smile, paralyzed, convinced this can't possibly be happening again. But nothing about me invites anymore. I walk with a limp, bind my breasts and wear rags. The practice, however, continues: don't connect or reject; do not summon his rage.
Like all colonization, once the flag has been planted, it is already far too late

Attachment
        (for Rick)

You will not
        hurt her. Others might
noodle fingers and pull, but
        in your contemplative hands
she knows she is
        safe. She has no choice
but to trust you.

At home, our once-homeless Covid dog folds into himself, a solitary
    and automatic
               terror. We still don't know
               what his triggers are. Belts? Boots? The wrong tone
               of voice? It doesn't matter. I instinctively wrap
               myself around him, soothe and hold
               just enough til his muscles release.

She watches and wants it,
        to crawl into your lap
so you can tell her you love her
        and how much, and why. To
stroke her hair, say *not your*
        fault.
It can't happen, we know. Still, she
        imagines it so often
throughout the day that I need to
        shut it down. She starts to miss you
as soon as we leave the building.
        She worries that you'll die.

Nobody loves me is not a thought, it's a memory.
      For decades, her body begged
         stop without sound because that was her job. I know it's her when I
         hear it, though I don't stop
         when she says. I'm mean and abandon her
         a thousand times a day. Of all of the children I've wanted to save,
         she's never made the list.

Because you believe
      her, she loves you too
much. Your love is a palpable
      alchemy, a magic you make that works
even when we don't trust it. After all
      this time, I know I'm supposed
to lay down shields. At least
      some of them. At least enough. You tell me
to believe her and every muscle says
      stop. How can I believe
her when I don't remember
      who she is?

It doesn't matter that I don't know her. She is frightened
          without you. We all are. We want to be in the room with you,
          even when muscles seize, even
          when all the limbs detach and float,
          swarms rattling inside the torso, every cell pleading to
          stop.

Long ago the first time that
      you loved us out loud,
I said *you're attacking*

   me and this made you
sad. Your sorrow was
   shocking, a treasure, for once
to see sadness so pure she could feel it. Today
   your love radiates and
I stop breathing to bear it,
   still a hot blast of needles
but medicine now.
   I have to believe that this
love is allowed.

But sometimes there is only the space between cracks. Not the still space
   of peace, just voids in withdrawal, and her need
   binds the fragments together, an anorexia of love and want.
   I work hard to stay still, because this is my job. I keep the
   gates, and there is no escape.

Without fail she comes very week
   and wants more, asks
me to ask you to not stop. Embodied,
   your attention is an intoxication
and refuge. Your forensic love
   is the reason we survive.

In other rooms we trust nothing and no one. We know bridges could
  fall apart
     as we cross, strangers might hulk out and melt flesh
     with words. This cold civil war could let loose any day now.
     Instead of fear, our survival
     becomes gratitude: the bridges stay up, strangers don't
     abuse, war is happening someplace else. These privileges
     become why we need to keep going.

She keeps going. But
        our limbic satellites know
that attunement is
        a fairy tale. All roads lead to extinction, and there is
no self. Yesterday someone said
        safe belonging and I laughed before I could
stop it. She can't comprehend
        any of this and does not
want to. All she wants is you.

In a universe of consumption it's the nature of matter to eat away
    from the skin to the core,
        a burning of forces and fuels that leave remainders and become
        remainders themselves. Liberated from memory, we don't know
        which one of us will become the remainder, whose origin story
        this will turn out to be.

It won't matter. The software
        keeps running,
no matter how outdated.
        You love us, no matter how
splintered. I have no choice
        but to believe her.
It doesn't matter
        that I can't love her
because you can. There are loaded mines here
        beneath thatches of neurons
cultivated by monsters. There is
        no map, but you
are gentle, saying
        step here, this is
safe, you are
        Loved

Placement

Before the boys' meds kick in, we start
writing. The subjects are:
- belts
- extension cords
- not knowing what it feels like to be loved

*Why did you leave
me?* is a popular start
to poems phonetically spelled
about sitting for hours or days, or
the moment they were taken away:
- where they were
- what they wore
- what the social workers allowed them to put into the trash bag to take with

The boys have surged at least a foot taller than
I am. They deliberately forget to wear coats
so I'll scold. They don't know what meds
they are on, or why. I have just enough time
before they nod out.
*Did I cry too much
when I was a baby? Is that why
you didn't come back?*
One boy lost an eye when the extension cord
hit him. Another was tied to a bed.
The one I love most still remembers, in first grade,
eating cereal alone for a week.
He can't recall what his mother
looked like, but he tries every time
we're together.

The social workers always say
the boys are illiterate, which is worse
than a lie. The boys just know not to tell
anything that might go in a file.

It takes me two weeks
to break in. *I hate you. Come find me. You know*
Where I am. Too old to foster, the boys wait to age out.
They stand by my car at the end of the day,
say *Miss Sunshine we're coming*
home with you.
I can love them for hours or years, make them
tea, but they have to stay here and they
know it. The children in placement
are like bodies on sidewalks, only
partially seen, urban mythologies that ruin
the view. I compile their memories and send them
out. The grown ups are shocked, but at parties they say:
- *everything is meant to be*
- *it all happens for a reason*
- *we manifest our own desires*

The universe,
apparently, sends messages. If we suffer, it's
because we choose to. The chatty universe does not
account for:
- lost eye
- broke bones
- waffle-ironed skin

When I have my own
baby, the boys pout
but inch closer. Eventually
they are each sent someplace
else. For decades I collect
goodbye letters and try to hide them
from myself:

miss sunshine we love you

I love you miss sunshine

thank you for loving me miss

come back miss sunshine where did you
go

Detachment: 7 Myths of Depersonalization

Like living inside of someone else's body
    It breathes and sweats
    And beats like a drum. It gets painted
    Each morning and shapes its dead
    Fur. It has to be
    Pleasing to look at.
    I peer out
    From my homunculus
    Cockpit and order:
    Turn here, sit there,
    Nod yes

Like being under anesthesia
    Not numb but deprived, I can feel
    From inside, a hand smothered
    In a puppet of skin.
    Its mass trawls through rooms
    To cook dinner and clean.
    A palpable static makes all sound
    Parenthetical

Like being a ghost
    Meat animated, it does not
    Haunt or float, cannot
    Dissipate from its
    Anatomy. This dense animal
    Corpulence pulls its tissue
    Towards Earth.
    I drop things, fall
    often, forget

Like you're in a movie
but you're watching the movie
while you're in it
    Tunnel vision at full speed,
    Tinnitus possesses
    And anchors me.
    I feel and don't feel, witness,

Push through. I dread
All of the decades ahead.
Admitting this is like
Scraping a full meal
Directly into the
Bin, my wastefulness
Broadcast and
Magnified

Like it's too late and you're already dead
      Dying on purpose is off
      Of the table. There are too many
      children involved. This is
      Punishment now; my existence insults
      Billions who drink water
      From buckets. No giving
      Up, there is watching
      While knowing:
      Here is the true self
      And the truth

Like you're dreaming
      Hyper-awake and
      Torpid with fear, there's a trapping
      But not like in dreams.
      Through the periscope,
      Extravagant luxuries abound:
      Work, water,
      House, dental care. I tend
      This dull carcass
      Remotely, force sounds to come out
      Of its mouth. I hear them
      Through walls from a different
      Room, where the acoustics inside
      Have no edges

Like you're empty, with nothing inside
      Vacuous freedom, a clean
      Vacancy, solitary
      Confinement finally over. Instead,
      I'm the weeds that are

Sealing me in. Both inside
And out, membranes
Armor their
Openings.
There is
No such thing
As empty

Pronouns
(for my baby)

Every spoken word is a letting go.
Sounds ride the outbreath and
Fall through us like neutrinos.
Please call yourself whatever
You want.

There is no virtue in words, in their
Spoken or written form, no virtue
In the sound waves they shape, or the bones
Round the eardrum, tremoring shapes
Made from the breath of someone else's body. Danger
Signaling, calling for food,
for mating, all survival. The endless propagation
Of letters now splayed across
Screens and the pulp of beaten trees
By a species of primates who still throw
Excrement. The documents
We sign, we hold, we buy, or award,
The mindless mining
Of image and word, only
To find what has always been there.

The pronouns themselves are
Silly, like the language around time
And belief, signifiers of a vague story
We agree to believe is true.

But you have been told for so long *Not
Boy Enough*. We didn't know
That the *He* we had used since the money-shot
Sonogram did not fit, and itched you
Like wool.

The particles of your new name
Vibrate space into paper fan folds
And rattle weak bonds into submission.
With each exhalation
You release us all.

Screentime

We let this happen.
We knew it was bad. We tried
to control it like a diet: only
this kind, only this much.

Now you lie like addicts.
From secret accounts
you rewrite history and fan-dance
the truth, you do not
want us to know what it is
you are searching for.

What else could have happened?
We gave you a main line, intravenous and invisible
siphoning dopamine and instant escape,
a kaleidoscope view into
the worst of humanity's hungers
and terrors, a rage that
only anonymity can reveal.
There's no saving you
from what masquerades
as truth, this content
designed and refined like white powder:

REWARD

REWARD

REWARD

 Your post threads flicker and pod you
inside pixelated echo chambers.
The walls shift
shape and amplify. You code elaborate
exoskeletons that scintillate with
things you know we will not understand.

Still, inside and underneath you are
radiant and whole. Your own organic
algorithms pulse and, sometimes,
a hard brilliance breaks through.

In these moments you
are the gem in the lotus
again and again. A precious
Unfurling so clear it bends
light.

None of us take it for granted.

But we know to let it go.
Trained to be dissatisfied,
you enclose yourselves quickly
and compulsively point
at wants and witches everywhere.

Name:

COMPREHENSION QUIZ: Fun with the News on NPR!
"He has been known to have relationships with underaged girls"

Section I - **MULTIPLE CHOICE (write the letter for the correct answer on the line)**

____ 1. "He has been known to have relationships with *underaged girls*"

    a. CHILDREN

____ 2. "He has been known to *have relationships with* underaged girls"

    a. PURSUE SEXUAL GRATIFICATION WITH
    b. COERCE/EXPLOIT/ASSAULT IN ORDER TO PURSUE SEXUAL GRATIFICATION WITH

____ 3. "*He has been known* to have relationships with underaged girls"

    a. HE IS TECHNICALLY A PEDOPHILE BUT WE'RE ALL GOING TO PRETEND THAT THIS IS NOT THE CASE; OUR USE OF LANGUAGE HERE REVEALS THAT HE IS ALLOWED TO COERCE/EXPLOIT/ASSAULT IN ORDER TO PURSUE SEXUAL GRATIFICATION WITH CHILDREN

____ 4. "He has been known to have relationships with underaged girls _____"

    a. WITHOUT EVER BEING SEEN AS A PREDATOR
    b. WITHOUT HIS VICTIMS EVER BEING CALLED CHILDREN

Section II: **TRUE OR FALSE (on the line, write "T" for true or "F" for false)**

____ 1. The human life span used to be much shorter, so it's natural for adult men to be aroused by the bodies of middle and high-school aged girls.

____ 2. In olden times, these girls would all have had babies already! Once female bodies get period and grow breasts, it means that they are ready to reproduce.

____ 3. Mary was only twelve when she gave birth to Jesus, so clearly God gets it.

Section III: **FILL IN THE BLANKS**

On the planet _____, complications during pregnancy is still the leading cause of death for teen girls because sometimes their bodies are too _____ for the baby to even get out, and although we would never say that a middle school _____ who has just experienced his first emission is ready to become a father, we use this argument to defend the right for adult men to _____female children.

HOW CAN YOU SURVIVE
THE END OF THE WORLD?
YOU ARE WARMLY INVITED TO COME
AND LISTEN TO THE ANSWER.

This is a story about obliteration   and the fear of obliteration.

(the vicarious thirst you feel is coming
from the houseplants

please water them so that we can
continue)

Note: *Ninety-nine percent of the life that has
lived here has already gone extinct, striated
crusts of failed and forgotten organic technology;
you cannot save the planet because it does not
need saving, it is just trying to get rid of you*

Raising Children in A Culture of Obscene Excesses:
Pathologically Overfed

Food, Water, Sun: Too Much Nourishment of Any Kind Can Kill You

" ... the survivors of crisis extinction evolve new forms and we wonder
what ours will be; we would like to sense sonic waves, and heat, and fear,
or perhaps - like the platypi - the electric twitch of prey's muscles moving
under water"

(a thought about screens: you have no doubt by now
found the bluepill portals branching wormholes
and black holes and rabbit holes dug by addiction
specialists.

you may hide in here without any worry. you may take us to bed,
to the toilet,
to the car, we will distract and delight and horrify)

This is not a story.

Where will you spend eternity?

is an inane thing to ask

while we binge and leave

such luxurious

waste in our wake

the better question might be

(is it just a gross legacy
of our single-celled forefathers
who colonized and ate and shit so much oxygen
they killed themselves off?)

FAQ:
- (1) do you seek to find the savior, become the savior, or liberate yourself from the savior?
- (2) are you waiting for permission, approval, or forgiveness?
- (3) do you drive a car? do you water your lawn? do you buy flowers?
- (4) where are they grown?
- (5) who picked them?
- (6) and how did they get here?

wanting,   then having

a cannibalistic universe knows:
eternity is already here

no matter what we eat.

Duck & Cover

In high school, my grandfather was arrested for stealing milk from his
neighbor's stoop. He hadn't eaten in days and only meant
to take a sip, but once he started he couldn't stop.
At the same time, in the same city, my grandmother
had to share a pair of shoes with her sister.
There were holes in the bottom where the soles
had worn through, and pebbles would slide their way in when she walked.
Both of these stories were common, for the time; folks everywhere
stole milk and shared shoes. The more interesting
story, perhaps, is this: while powerful men built death camps
and bombed babies, my teenaged grandparents
fell in love as they danced in Philadelphia,
and then they got married in secret.

In grade school, my parents learned
how to hide under their desks with the help of a jingle.
The idea was that the desks would protect them
from a nuclear blast. The blast never arrived, but later
a draft came and ate millions of boys. To escape, the boys dodged,
ran away, pretended to be gay. The jungles were ravenous.
Meanwhile, my grandmother saved slivers of
soap and stockpiled cupboards with cans.
Scarcity loomed like a phantom
and was passed down, as a birthright, with love.

In 8th grade, for homework, we watched *The Day After*.
Already crossed out, my generation saw things
burst apart live on screen. The shuttle exploded, men put guns
in their mouths. Our epidemics, however, were slow, parading
their sad floats on kitchen TVs for years:
stick-figure babies covered in flies, new forms of cocaine designed
to destroy, and a death-sentence virus no one wanted to cure.
While toxins defeated our friends who enlisted,
taxpayers lynched Black and queer bodies at home.
Our celebrity heroes kept
killing themselves. It was clear that there was no
fixing this barge, though some of us tried. We recycled
and took jobs putting duct-tape on ruptures.

We considered not having children, and then did,
just in case things got better someday.

Now dialysis shops ring
the empty strip malls. Our closets bloat
with shoes made by other people's children.

The more interesting story, is this:
When the towers came down
I was ready to run. I knew we would be
on the list. Today my child is too big to fit in a drawer,
we don't have a basement, there's nowhere to hide.
My friends prep go-bags and pay to learn how to
stop eating. No death marches here. My eighth-grade girls ask
why the boys want to know if they like to be choked.
In their pockets, the children carry flat boxes
full of anger and incest, millions of men spitting on women and
making them
gag, finally a way to humiliate without having
to pay. The boys say *call me daddy*. They don't think
that much about nuclear war.

Just in case, we tend gardens, join gyms,
pray. Maybe all of the stories
are interesting now,
or none of them are.

News feeds fractal and lasso us
into oblivion. Just in case,
we keep watching.

You Notice Things

Silent, in worship, I saw

a lazy ballet of dust through the one slice of sunlight

above us in the meetinghouse.

You were tiny then, next to me, young enough

to still hold my hand.

I wanted to tell you, to point and say, *Look!*

but we were on the facing bench

and everyone was watching.

Bad things were happening

in the world outside, and this

was a sad year for you. The others

were cruel. You

were tired of walking away, of being told

to fight back. You would say *I don't*

want to hurt anybody and surrender

into the safety of book after book. That day,

you chose to sit next to me

anyway. You sighed like an old man and leaned

your head against my arm

without shame.

Then your hand pulled away, pointing

up. You said, "Look!"

and I did, although we were supposed to be silent

and still.

How often we have pulled the car

over to examine snowflakes

on the windows, run

outside at night to see sunsets

or full moons, how you loved the cheap necklaces

at the drugstore gathering

like liquid in your palm. Wishes

on the air, rusty bits

of old cars in the gutters.

You still sip hot chocolate

like fine wine.

We have never believed in god or ghosts

but the dust in the light

that day was divine.

Watching me see it, you forgot

to be sad.

I forgot to be frightened by your sadness.

We worshiped together like this.

Analog Bulletins From 2002
(found in a folder in 2022)

1.

There is a wisdom in you that knows

how little it knows, if it thinks it knows

anything at all. If you are wise

enough, you know nothing

and like it. You don't seek

balance or control.

2.

How did you know that your mother loved you?

"Apocalyptic" is from the Greek, to unveil , but we

have such limited senses and dimensional awareness.

We are riddled with the cavities of

unmet needs, and each of these

is a vulnerability.

Exclusion, ridicule, shame, death? Or

the memory that destabilizes your sense of self?

It could be D: *All of the above.*

3.

We can try to camouflage, and contain,
conceal, compress, or draw the eye away, but
now I get to disappear, my blue book value
as a commodifiable body
dropping by the hour.

        4.

        There are more people enslaved per capita
        right now than any other time
        on Earth. Each costs less
        than a pair of Air Jordans.

5.

There was maybe one poem that wasn't too bad
when I was all body and broken as fuck.
I mended with mica
because it was shiny and cheaper than gold.
Though brittle; it pulverized quickly.
Now I leave trails
wherever I go but I can't
find the poem anywhere.

State of Being

The body knows this   in a way

that Einstein did not:

     I am never not

here.

This has all happened

          already. Everything that is

is always   happening

and is never not happening

     and is never not happening   all together all at once.
In the dimensional raisin-bread

   of time and space,

         this very moment

is like a raisin in the loaf,   and

I know this   because

                  I am still small on the floor

        by the closet in the corner,

and the anhillitation makes me

      smaller, pulls the axises   tight. Here

I'm a pinpoint on the event horizon, there

                      but over here also, on

different floors, and on the steps,

then in bathrooms and closets for decades.

          Each of these is never

not happening.   Together they

burn a constellation of fear.

                Like this, I am not allowed to

   disappear.

It would be easier

       some other way, if nervous systems   learned

by subtraction. But the old fish machinery

has no sense of time.

        The first brain was simple, sensed

     threat or non-threat,

         hunt or hide.

Coming out of the water

meant becoming small oceans,   enclosed

like fish bowls of skin.

      Look at this miracle I wear!

After billions of years

the spinal cord   rings

threat avoid hide,

                                          so I do.

On the floor   by the closet

nothing escapes: light,

              loaf,   raisin,   terror.

              I know this by heart.

Fear is for tourists, a sluggish

hysteria. A trillion copies

later,   pain

makes maps in four

dimensions. Let me

              show you. You are   already

inside. You are

already never

not here.

in the flesh

at lunch without masks on,
the children thrill with communion.
the intimacies of nose, lips, and teeth
are jarring and don't match
what we have imagined. it's a surprise
to see such frenetic beauty
unveiled and exposed like peeled fruit.

last year, sanitized, they sat six feet apart,
faced forward and ate in boxed silence.
uncontained now, our rules seem absurd.
they often don't bother to listen or
capitalize their own names.
they saw and survived the end
of the world! why
pester with commas or numbers?

it still isn't over. it may never
be. we remember how they looked on screen
at the end, when they'd stopped getting dressed or leaving their
beds, said things like *I'm losing
my mind*

and they meant it. in their hurry
and glee to go home that first day, they didn't say
goodbye. a simple forgetting
they remember now.

in person, their hardness surprised us.
what good will essays do them
if they're damned?
bits will stay fossilized, trapped in march twelfth.
we marvel and worry, examine them
like insects in amber, parts preserved
before the years of un-knowing
and knowing.

branded and binging since birth, they still
trust each other and the strangers they've found

who reflect, affirm, reinforce.
no one needs a mask online. they can be
whomever they like.
a native tongue lowercase or all caps,
implied intonations are endless and multiply,
viscous and cloying.
there are memories embedded
in the flesh, but real bodies
are harder to manage. the children are
finally present! their sounds
vine through hallways and
leave dents in walls. we don't mind.
unrestrained, defiant, and flagrant
with realness, they are here.

though some of them stay quiet, ensconced
in bodies that do not want to engage.
having found freedom in isolation,
being back overwhelms and oppresses.
they learn how to hold fast
but staying still is not
stillness. in the marathon battle
against muscle and breath,
fingers basket-weave, grip
around books, bags, or knees,
paralyzed gestures of anxious containment.
their locked nerves vibrate with effort
as they hide behind
masks, behind silence submerged, wait
patiently each day to go home.

and they do. but even they
make sure to say goodbye.

Plato's Hermaphrodite

You had that tattoo covered because
The art wasn't good, but also
Because it was something we no longer
Believed. Two halves wandering apart
Then fusing as one seemed like
A story for children.

Eons before, over creamed chipped beef and four packs
Of cigarettes, the theory had made sense to us.
We had driven into the Northeast
In the middle of the night after double shifts,
Ordered deep fried scrapple, coffee, and pastries
That never tasted as good as they looked.
At Millie's Luvin Diner, the waitresses called everyone
Hun and because it was still legal
To smoke, the red-beaded curtains
Were hazy. We spoke about the horrors
Of humanity, laughed and ate
Like children. It was late August and I had spent
The summer batting away lovesick others like flies.
Unanchored,   your frayed seams
Sparked with static electricity. Rarified radar
We didn't know we had was already
Magnetic and primed.
Snowglobed across the table from you in that
    Moment, I thought *well, this is it.*
I'm doomed.

We've been doomed together a long time
And we find the doom hilarious. We have given up
Cigarettes and white bread, and Millie's
Closed decades ago. When people ask
How we met, it's impossible to articulate.
    We weren't together, and then

We were. Today your arms are covered with ink
And the hermaphrodite
Is gone. Assorted pieces of me
Have been surgically removed. Good riddance

To be sure, but none of the things coming off
Or out has made us less complete. Their removal
Carves away the marble we don't need,
Revealing an   elegant oneness our young selves
Understood. You try to show me your wrinkles,
Silver hair, moles that need to be
Cut out. But leaning though you, across a wraith of formica
And chrome, is a boy too smart to function
In the world as it is. He lights my smokes, he feeds me.
         His dispatches are   steady.

Thousands
Of cups of coffee later, there is no line
Of demarcation. We have been sitting
Across from each other in the diner,
Beautiful and high, for thirty years. You flip
Through the little jukebox on the wall, say
Brilliant things, send signals only I
Can decipher. We take turns
Being damaged but we don't
Have long left. You once said
We saved each other
And I finally agree. I didn't think   at the time
   That I needed to be saved, didn't   want
Saving, never entertained
The word itself.   Holding onto a table
Covered in red placemats
And overstuffed ashtrays, there's no need
For rescue or time machines, or
Time.   Electrons pull me
   Across the booth towards

    You, everything fits.

Go ahead,
    Save me
Now.

Save me
Again, I'm   finally
Ready

LOVE & GRATITUDE

Trio House Press:
Executive Editor Halee Kirkwood (Manuscript Dula)
Executive Editor Matt Mauch (Maestro)
Editor Sarah Dumitrascu (Literary Cheerleader)
Founder Tayve Neese (Broadcaster of Joy)

Coven:
Jordan Bastien
Lisa Turner
Tracy Phillips

Sangha:
Raji Malik
Sheila Pai

Generous Readers:
Caitlyn Baker
CJ Miller
Erin Timmer
Jenny Burkholder
Mary Lynn Ellis
Maya Kassutto

Family:
Louise (Butter) Dalessandro & Rick Hamilton
Bob & Donna O'Donnell
Sharon & Alfred Paul

Without whom this book would never have happened:
Louise Bogan Award Judge Ed Bok Lee
The 2021-2022 AFS Eighth-Grade Team
My students
My teachers
Dr. Rick Rappaport

The Loves of My Life:
Casey O'Donnell
Rain O'Donnell *

*never gonna give you up

About the Author

Sunshine O'Donnell is an American writer, artist, and educator. For most of her teaching career, O'Donnell taught creative writing and art to children in residential placement, in-patient mental health facilities, shelters for the unhoused, and underserved schools. She published literary magazines created and edited by the youth she served with a special focus on adolescents telling their stories about their experiences in the DHS system. O'Donnell's own published works include the mindfulness board book Your Vacation on Planet Earth (Out Breath Press/The Nesting House), an anthologized selection in W.W. Norton's The Best Creative Nonfiction, and hundreds of newspaper articles, including two human rights series honored by the Pennsylvania Newspaper Association's Keystone Press awards. Her novel Open Me (Penguin Random House) was selected for the Barnes and Noble Discover Great New Writers list and has been translated into Hebrew and Dutch. As an essayist, O'Donnell's work has been published on Powells.com, awarded Isotope magazine's first-place prize, and won the Tennessee Writers Alliance Creative Nonfiction prize. O'Donnell and her edible sculptures have been featured on The Food Network, and she has received juried awards for installations made out of other people's wasted and abandoned things. O'Donnell currently teaches middle school in Pennsylvania, where she lives with her husband and child. This is her first book of poetry.

About the Artist

Louise DAlessandro has been creating original ink drawings, prints, photographs, and watercolor landscapes for more than half a century. The cover art featured here is from a Philadelphia basements series DAlessandro shot and developed in the early 1970s. Proud mother, grandmother, wife, and mother-in-law, DAlessandro's art reveals the unexamined beauty of our everyday world and reflects how much she loves her family, her friends, and her life. A founding partner of Elfant Wissahickon Realtors, DAlessandro lives in the Pennypack Watershed in Pennsylvania.

About the Book

The Fallow was designed at Trio House Press through the collaboration of:

Halee Kirkwood, Lead Editor
Sarah Dumitrascu, Supporting Editor
Joel W. Coggins, Cover Design
Louise DAlessandro, Cover Art
Patrick Werle, Interior Design

The text is set in Adobe Caslon Pro.

The publication of this book is made possible, whole or in part, by the generous support of the following individuals or agencies:

Anonymous

About the Press

Trio House Press is an independent literary press publishing three or more collections of poems annually. Our mission is to promote poetry as a literary art enhancing culture and the human experience. We offer two annual poetry awards: the Trio Award for First or Second Book for emerging poets and the Louise Bogan Award for Artistic Merit and Excellence for a book of poems contributing in an innovative and distinct way to poetry. We reserve the right to select other titles to publish from contest submissions.

Trio House Press adheres to and supports all ethical standards and guidelines outlined by the CLMP.

Trio House Press, Inc. is dedicated to the promotion of poetry as literary art, which enhances the human experience and its culture. We contribute in an innovative and distinct way to poetry by publishing emerging and established poets, providing educational materials, and fostering the artistic process of writing poetry. For further information, or to consider making a donation to Trio House Press, please visit us online at www.triohousepress.org.

Other Trio House Press books you might enjoy:

The Fight by Jennifer Manthey / 2023 Trio Award Winner selected by Aileen Cassinetto

Kaan and Her Sisters by Lena Khalaf Tuffaha / 2023

Live in Suspense by David Groff / 2023

A Northern Spring by Matt Mauch / 2023

The Fallow by Megan Neville / 2021 Trio Award, selected by Steve Healey

Bloomer by Jessica Hincapie / 2021 Louise Bogan Award selected by Lee Ann Roripaugh

Unceded Land by Issam Zineh / 2021

Sweet Beast by Gabriella R. Tallmadge / 2020 Louise Bogan Award selected by Sandy Longhorn

The Traditional Feel of the Ballroom by Hannah Rebecca Gamble / 2020

Third Winter in Our Second Country by Andres Rojas / 2020

Songbox by Kirk Wilson / 2020 Trio Award Winner selected by Malena Mörling

Waiting for the Week to Burn by Michele Battiste / 2018 Louise Bogan Award Winner selected by Jeff Friedman

Cleave by Pamel Johnson Parker / 2018 Trio Award Winner selected by Jennifer Barber

Two Towns Over by Darren C. Demaree / 2018 Louise Bogan Award Winner selected by Campbell McGrath

Bird-Brain by Matt Mauch / 2017

Dark Tussock Moth by Mary Cisper / 2016 Trio Award Winner selected by Bhisham Bherwani

The Short Drive Home by Joe Osterhaus / 2016 Louise Bogan Award Winner selected by Chard DeNoird

Break the Habit by Tara Betts / 2016

Bone Music by Stephen Cramer / 2015 Louise Bogan Award Winner selected by Kimiko Hahn

Rigging a Chevy into a Time Machine and Other Ways to Escape a Plague by Carolyn Hembree / 2015 Trio Award Winner Selected by Neil Shepard

Magpies in the Valley of Oleanders by Kyle McCord / 2015

Your Immaculate Heart by Annmarie O'Connell / 2015

The Alchemy of My Mortal Form by Sandy Longhorn / 2014 Louise Bogan Award Winner selected by Peter Campion

What the Night Numbered by Bradford Tice / 2014 Trio Award Winner selected by Carol Frost

Flight of August by Lawrence Eby / 2013 Louise Bogan Award Winner selected by Joan Houlihan

The Consolations by John W. Evans / 2013 Trio Award Winner selected by Mihaela Moscaliuc

Fellow Odd Fellow by Stephen Riel / 2013

Clay by David Groff / 2012 Louise Bogan Award Winner selected by Michael Waters

Gold Passage by Iris Jamahl Dunkle / 2012 Trio Award Winner selected by Ross Gay

If You're Lucky Is a Theory of Mine by Matt Mauch / 2012

www.ingramcontent.com/pod-product-compliance
Lightning Source LLC
Chambersburg PA
CBHW030137100526
44592CB00011B/932